every teenager's
little black book
on how to get along
with your parents

by blaine bartel

every teenager's
little black book
on how to get along
with your parents

by blaine bartel

Harrison House
Tulsa, Oklahoma

08 07 06 05   10 9 8 7 6 5 4

*Every Teenager's Little Black Book on
How To Get Along With Your Parents*
ISBN 1-57794-626-X
Copyright © 2004 by Blaine Bartel
P.O. Box 691923
Tulsa, Oklahoma 74179

Published by Harrison House, Inc.
P.O. Box 35035
Tulsa, Oklahoma 74153

contents

Freedom

Communication

contents (continued)

contents (continued)

Chores

Strategies

[FREEDOM]

2 THINGS FREEDOM IS NOT

I was preaching at a crusade, and a young man walked up to me after the evening's events and said, "I don't listen to anyone. I do what I want, when I want, with who I want to do it. I'm free!" I looked at him, trying to think of a way to shock him back into reality, and said, "Is that right? Well, I'm going to take that girl on your arm away from you tonight, and if you try to stop me, I'll drop kick you right in the face!" Of course, I wasn't serious…just setting up a point. He looked back and said, "Hey, you can't do that. That's wrong man, to steal a guy's girl!" I smiled and said, "Hey, you're the one who said freedom is doing whatever you want, whenever you want, and I'm free too!" He got the point…which brings us to 2 things freedom is not.

1. **Freedom is not a life without boundaries.** Ask any prison inmate how much freedom they are enjoying after living outside the boundaries of the law.

2. **Freedom is not getting away from your parents.** Authority exists wherever you go, and you best learn to respect it. Your parents will likely be the kindest, most forgiving authority you'll ever have.

2 MISTAKES TEENAGERS MAKE
IN A DESIRE FOR FREEDOM

I once heard a comedienne from the '70s and '80s make this proud statement: "The trouble with being in a rat race is that if you win the race, you're still a rat." The point is, you don't have to sneak, lie, and demand to get your way in life. Freedom attained by force and deception will be short-lived. Here are 2 critical mistakes young people make in their quest for living freely.

1. **Comparing your freedoms to the freedoms of others.** Have you ever said something like, "Well, all my friends get to do this. How come I'm the only one who can't?" The trap of comparisons will never end if you give in to it early in life. Learn to be content with the good things you already have.

2. **Getting your freedom by deception.** For example, telling your mom you're going one place and going somewhere else, the place she wouldn't let you go in the first place. Maybe you won't get caught, but you still have to live with yourself and your lies. And all your friends will know you can't be trusted—you'll deceive your own mother if necessary. The Bible says that the truth will set you free. (James 8:31.) Truthfulness brings trust, and trust secures freedom.

7 THINGS A PARENT LOVES IN A TEENAGER

The Bible tells us that a wise child will make one's father happy, but a foolish child will cause one's mother grief. (Prov. 10:1.) The attitudes and actions you can display in your home have a major influence on the happiness of your family.

Here are 7 things you can do to bring joy in your family.

1. Do your chores without someone asking you to do them.

2. Offer to help with something around the house that is not usually your responsibility.

3. Think of a compliment you can give your mom, dad, or both.

4. Ask your parents if there is anything you can do to improve your behavior.

5. When asked to do something, don't procrastinate even a minute—go right to it.

6. If you have a brother or sister, treat your sibling with the same respect that you would want in return.

7. Be polite, thoughtful, and helpful outside of your home, at school, and in other activities.

3 FREEDOMS YOU ARE ENTITLED
TO EVERY DAY

Men and women have given their lives so that you and I can enjoy the life we have today. The freedom we enjoy in America is stained with the blood of soldiers who died for the rights we often take for granted. God sent His Son, Jesus, to give us eternal freedoms that no one can take away from you. Here are 3 freedoms that you might fight to keep.

1. **The freedom to worship God.** I've had students whose parents have told them they couldn't go to church and be a Christian. I've told those students that they must obey their higher authority—God Almighty—and to respectfully explain to their parents that they have made a decision to live for Christ and cannot retreat.

2. **The freedom to share your faith.** More and more in America, ungodly groups of people are trying to limit the expression of faith in any public venue. It won't be long until they try to tell us what we can do in our own homes! In spite of their efforts, we have the God-given right to proclaim the goodness of God to all people wherever we go. (Mark 16:15.)

3. **The freedom to learn.** There are many countries around the world whose citizens are told what they are allowed to learn. Many have no libraries, no communication tools, no higher education. You have been given the right to discover all that you need to make your life all that it can be. Use it!

3 SACRIFICES THAT WILL
GUARANTEE FREEDOM

You can get a lot of things for free in life. Those AOL CDs at the grocery store. Mints at a restaurant. Real estate booklets at the convenience store. But one thing I can promise you is not free are freedoms. There is work and sacrifice you must make to gain new freedom. This is true with your parents, with your work career, or with any other area of life. Here are 3 sacrifices you must be willing to make.

1. **The sacrifice of honesty.** Even when it hurts you, honesty must be a value you hold true to. When you develop a reputation for always being honest, even when it's to your detriment, people will trust you with freedoms not afforded to others.

2. **The sacrifice of diligence.** When your parents see you do your homework, yard work, chores, or part-time job well and without complaints, your freedoms will rise.

3. **The sacrifice of servanthood.** Stop demanding your rights, and start serving others' requests. When you develop a heart that is "others first," others will start to put "you first."

[COMMUNICATION]

3 THINGS YOU MUST TELL YOUR PARENTS

Communication is the key to victory in any kind of relationship. Great companies, great armies, great churches, great sports teams, and great homes all have one thing in common: They have learned to communicate effectively with one another. Communication is not talking. It is listening, observing, studying, and finally, talking. People who only learn to talk are not communicating; they are spewing. In opening up good communication lines with your parents, there are 3 things you must always tell them.

1. **Tell them when you need help.** It may be in school, a relationship, or a job, but if you need help and guidance, let your parents know. That's why God gave them to you—to help you get through tough times.

2. **Tell them when you've made a mistake.** It might be easier at the time to try to cover it up, but honesty will not only help you to not make this same mistake again, it will also earn you big points in the "trust" quest.

3. **Tell them you love and appreciate them.** Sure, there's no such thing as a perfect parent, but most all have made a very significant investment of time, energy, and money in their children. Regularly let them know you love them, even if they don't always show the same love in return.

2 THINGS NEVER TO TELL YOUR PARENTS

My wife, Cathy, and I have had the privilege of raising 3 wonderful boys, who, at the writing of this book, are all teenagers, and one has graduated. They have not been faultless and neither have we, but in spite of the challenges that come in any family, we are very, very close to them. All 3 of my sons would honestly say that Dad is their best friend. To their credit, there are 2 things they have never told me—and you shouldn't tell your parents these things either.

1. **Never tell your parents you hate them.** You may disagree, be annoyed, or become a little irritated, but the word *hate* is a terrible word that can break the spirit and will of the strongest person. Take it out of your vocabulary, except when talking about sin and the devil.

2. **Never tell your parents you wish you weren't born.** Maybe life has been hard. Perhaps you haven't had the breaks that other kids in your school have enjoyed. But remember this: God created you, and He made you for a purpose. Oftentimes, kids who rise above a difficult upbringing become a great success because of things they learned.

7 QUESTIONS TO ASK YOUR PARENTS

IN THE NEXT 7 DAYS

Asking questions is a great way to learn and grow. You gain a perspective on areas of your life that you may have never realized. Here are 7 questions to ask your parents in the next 7 days. Learn from each answer.

1. How can I be a better son or daughter?

2. What do you see as my greatest strengths?

3. What do you think are the weaknesses that I must work on?

4. What friends do you see as the best influences in my life?

5. What kind of career could you see me getting into after

    I graduate?

6. When do I make you most proud?

7. What is the most important thing you've learned in life?

4 KEYS TO COMMUNICATING WELL

Have you ever got frustrated that someone didn't understand your side of an argument? Perhaps it was a result of not clearly and effectively communicating your point. I have made a living at being a good communicator. Organizations pay me thousands of dollars to communicate a message to their constituents. And I can tell you from experience, you must plan and prepare well if you are going to say anything that will be met with approval. Here are 4 keys for good personal communication.

1. **Think about things from the other person's perspective first.** This will help you to understand what they are going through, enabling you to respond more effectively.

2. **Write down your point or opinion in one sentence.** If you can't put it into one sentence, you will never make a convincing case for what you believe.

3. **Listen carefully to what the other person is saying.** You may learn something that you did not know that could change everything.

4. **Stay calm.** Don't cloud your message with outbursts and tirades of anger or emotion. Your point may be a good one, but you can lose the day with your attitude.

3 SECRETS OF A GOOD LISTENER

The Bible says in James 1:19 (NIV) that we are to "be quick to listen, slow to speak." Unfortunately, many people are just the opposite and are very quick to speak and extremely slow to listen. When you take the time to listen to somebody, you are showing them that you care and have respect for what they think. It will cement your relationship with that person. What does it take to be a good listener? Here are 3 secrets.

1. **Look into the eyes of the person you are listening to.** This, more than anything, says, "I really do care about what you have to say."

2. **Think about the point or concern they are making.** Don't be rehearsing in your mind your answer before you've fully caught all that they are communicating.

3. **Repeat back a brief synopsis of what they just told you.** For example, "Jim, I understand that you want to borrow $150 from me, but number one, I'm not a bank, and number two, I don't have an extra $150."

[ENTERTAINMENT]

3 REASONS YOUR MUSICAL CHOICES
ARE IMPORTANT

How many times have I heard teenagers tell me when referring to blatantly immoral messages in their music, "Well, Pastor Blaine, I don't listen to the words, so they don't affect me." I understand what they are trying to say, and I do believe you can make good choices in spite of listening to bad music. But there are 3 reasons good choices are critical for each of us.

1. **Messages, both good and evil, will have some effect on us.** Why? Because the Bible teaches that there is power in words. Proverbs 23:7 teaches that as a man thinks in his heart, so is he. We are a product of our thoughts, and our thoughts are influenced by what we listen to in music or anything else.

2. **Your witness and testimony for Christ are on the line each day.** If you are listening to music that is exalting fornication, murder, rebellion, etc., what does that say about your devotion to Christ to others around you?

3. **God's highest purpose for music is to facilitate worship and praise to Him in our lives.** That's why an important part of the menu of music on your I-POD or in your CD case should be music that glorifies God and inspires you to serve Him.

4 DANGER ZONES IN MODERN ENTERTAINMENT

I enjoy good entertainment just as much as the next guy, but I believe that we all must guard the gates of our minds and hearts. Second Timothy 3:1-6 says we are to have nothing to do with wicked and ungodly people. This biblical principle also applies to our entertainment.

Here are 4 danger zones that we must steer clear of in modern entertainment.

1. **Sexual immorality.** The Word of God says that there should not even be a hint of sexual immorality in our lives. (Eph. 5:3.) Have the courage not to compromise even when everyone else will.

2. **Disrespect for authority.** Honoring and obeying our parents will bring us blessings. (Ex. 20:12.) Paul

wrote that our police, military, and government leaders are ministers of God. (Rom. 13:6.)

3. **Mocking God.** Did you know that when you fail to react to others degrading God and godly principles, you come into agreement with those acts? Jesus said that if you're ashamed of Him and the Word, He will be ashamed of you. (Luke 9:26.)

4. **Rage.** Don't believe that uncontrolled anger will bring a solution to your problem. It won't. It will add to your already existing problems. Proverbs 14:16 (NIV) says, "A fool is hotheaded and reckless." Don't be a fool.

3 WAYS TO DEVELOP GOOD DISCERNMENT

I remember when I started out in the ministry as a youth evangelist back in the '80s. I did a "Rock Music Seminar," exposing a lot of the terrible lyrics that were in the music at that time. I played cuts off songs, had slides depicting evil-looking album covers—the whole deal! The problem was, I couldn't cover every teenager's music preferences in one night, and I was constantly having to update the seminar as new groups and artists were introduced and others faded. Rather than someone giving you a list of the good, the bad, and the ugly, it would be better for you to learn to discern what edifies and what doesn't for yourself. Here's how.

1. W.W.J.L.T. What would Jesus listen to? This is a great question to ask concerning anything in your music collection right now.

2. After listening to a certain group or artist, are you lifted up and inspired in all areas of life, including your faith in God?

3. The Word of God and the Holy Spirit. Is what you are listening to contradicting what God's Word teaches you, and is the Holy Spirit grieved by any of your choices?

5 WAYS TO HAVE A GREAT TIME
WITHOUT COMPROMISING

"Christians don't have any fun." That's the worst lie that's ever been pushed on young people in today's world! I've been a Christian since I was 16 years old, and I've had the time of my life the whole way. Let me give you 5 ways to get a life on the fast track.

1. **Reach out and make some great friends with similar interests.** Good friends can be a blast to hang out with. Laughing, talking, going places, learning how to live life together—it's awesome!

2. **Find a hobby or activity you love.** It may be a sport, collecting something, hunting, writing, acting, dancing—whatever. Just do something that you can look forward to.

3. **Learn how to throw a great party without drugs, alcohol, and sex.** A lot of Christian parties are boring because nothing is planned. It might be a great new game, karaoke, cooking everyone's favorite dish—just be creative!

4. **Get into trouble that doesn't hurt anyone.** It might be a great practical joke you and your friends play on somebody. Don't get me started. I love doing stuff like this!

5. **Make a list of things you've never done or tried and want to do.** Big stuff. Cool stuff. Now start making plans to check off everything on your list.

5 SCRIPTURES TO GUIDE YOUR
DAILY ENTERTAINMENT CHOICES

In evaluating things we watch, listen to, or do, it is important to allow God to help you with decisions by comparing your choices to God's instruction. Believe it or not, the Bible has a lot to say about entertainment. Here are 5 awesome Scriptures to use in all your evaluations.

1. "Finally, brethren, whatever things are true, whatever things are noble, whatever things are just, whatever things are pure, whatever things are lovely, whatever things are of good report, if there is any virtue and if there is anything praiseworthy—meditate on these things" (Phil. 4:8). What kind of thoughts is this producing in your life?

2. "And do not be conformed to this world, but be transformed by the renewing of your mind, that you may prove what is that good and acceptable and perfect will of God" (Rom. 12:2). Is this causing you to conform to a worldly attitude or behavior?

3. "According to the eternal purpose which He accomplished in Christ Jesus our Lord" (Eph. 3:11). Does it fall in line with God's purpose for your life?

4. "It is better to hear the rebuke of the wise, than for a man to hear the song of fools" (Eccl. 7:5). The Bible says a fool says, "There is no God." Is your entertainment denying the existence or goodness of God?

5. "And the tongue is a fire, a world of iniquity. The tongue is so set among our members that it defiles the whole body, and sets on fire the course of nature; and

it is set on fire by hell" (James 3:6). The tongue has power to destroy with the words it speaks. What kind of words are you allowing into your spirit?

2 REASONS FOR RULES

Rules are never a big bundle of fun when you are a teenager. It seems like at every turn you're met with another barrier that keeps you from experiencing all that life can bring. Can I let you in on a little secret? You don't want to experience *all* that life can bring. For many people, life brings a lot of pain, hurt, and tragedy. Oftentimes, this pain is a result of getting outside the boundaries. Understanding this will help you in seeing the reasons for rules.

1. **Somewhere, someone cared about you enough to create a boundary.** It is illegal in hockey to carry your stick up high when going into the corner with another player to secure the puck. That rule was created by an official somewhere who cared about my head, because I'm a hockey player!

2. **Your teenage years are a time to develop good habits and safe boundaries.** Without boundaries, our lives would run wild during our teenage years. It's a time of stepping out and learning things that we've never known before as children. Driving powerful automobiles. Going places without Mom or Dad. Feeling the emotions of romantic love for the first time. The list goes on. Without solid, consistent, guiding hearts and hands over our life, trouble would be imminent.

3 KEYS TO A COMMANDMENT

This whole "rules" thing got started a long time ago with Almighty God. Moses came down from a mountain with 10 commandments from God. When lived by, the children of Israel had great victory. When forgotten, they suffered horrendous defeats at the hands of their enemies. But there is more to God's commandments than meet the eye. Let's look at the commandment "Thou shalt not steal" and see 3 keys to every rule God has given us.

1. **We must know the *Person* behind the commandment.** If God tells us not to steal, then we can trust Him as an important Person in our world not to steal from us. He won't break His own commandment. You can trust God. He's on your side!

2. **We must know the *principle* behind the commandment.** The principle He wants us to learn from "Thou shalt not steal" is respect. If you respect someone, you won't take what belongs to him. If you fail to respect others, you will quickly lose your own respect.

3. **We must know the *power* behind the commandment.** If God asks us to abide by one of His guidelines for living, He is obligated to provide the ability to live it out. That's why it's important to stay in relationship with God through His Son, Jesus. God promises to work in you to perform His will and pleasure. (Phil. 2:13.)

4 SECRETS OF RENEGOTIATING

I want to be careful here, because there are some rules that simply aren't open for renegotiation. I trust you have rules in your home that prohibit premarital sex, drugs and alcohol, and killing your little brother. These can never change. But there are some rules that your parents may be open to adjusting down the road—curfews, chores, and new choices that maturity will allow you to make on your own. As a father of 3 teenagers, let me give you 4 little secrets.

1. **Start with a good track record.** Don't expect a lot of new freedom if you haven't been performing well under the current regime!

2. **Don't go in with a list of demands.** You're not a free agent with a lot of other options! Tread softly,

ask humbly, and show appreciation for what you
already have.

3. **Think through your approach.** Give good reasons
   why you feel you've earned some new freedom, and
   explain how you will handle it with responsibility.

4. **Keep a great attitude if the answer is no.** By
   not throwing a temper tantrum, this will prove to your
   parents even more that you are starting to act like an
   adult. With the right attitude, the answer could be yes a
   little ways down the road!

6 THINGS TO KNOW BEFORE YOU
BREAK THE LAW

The Bible says in Romans 13:1-2 that every person should be subject to a governing authority and that our resisting that authority will bring judgment on us. Here are 6 things you should know if you break the law, whether it is exceeding a speed limit or taking something that belongs to someone else.

1. God is bound by His Word to back up those who establish the laws, not you.

2. Even if you are not caught immediately, the consequences will eventually catch up with you.

3. Know what living on the inside of a 4' x 6' prison cell feels like, because that will be your future home.

4. Go down to the local jail and meet the criminals. If you choose to break the law, they could be your best friends.

5. Get a job making 50 cents an hour. That's about what they'll pay you in prison.

6. Realize that smaller violations will slowly but surely lead you to larger ones. It will become a downward spiral that is difficult to recover from.

3 DANGERS OF HANGING OUT WITH FRIENDS WHO HAVE NO RULES

I'm convinced that many teenagers don't want to break their parents rules, but they allow their friends to do it for them. Proverbs 13:20 warns us that if we walk with wise people, we will be wise ourselves, but walking with fools will result in destruction. Remember that when you are choosing a friend, you are doing more than finding a new companion. You are choosing their lifestyle, and for better of for worse, they will influence you.

1. **The danger of decision-making.** When making important decisions outside of your home and family, you better have friends in your life who won't put you at risk. Bad friends will help you make bad decisions.

2. **The danger of deception.** Dangerous friends won't tell you the truth about things like sex, drinking, or getting high. Their thoughts never go past the spur of the moment. The problem is, one dangerous moment can lead to a lifetime of destruction.

3. **The danger of damnation.** Friends don't let friends go to hell. The Bible warns us against being unequally yoked with a person who doesn't believe and act like a Christian. (2 Cor. 6:14.) Your eternal soul is too high a cost for a friend you might think is cool.

[CHORES]

3 REASONS TO HELP YOUR PARENTS

It's your parents' house, right? It's their yard, their dishes,
their cars and windows and carpet. So why should kids have
to work on all this stuff? After all, what are children
anyways—free labor?! Aren't there laws against this? The
truth is, you use all this stuff too, and there are 3 reasons you
owe it to Mom and Dad to help take care of it.

1. Good parents have a responsibility to teach their child
    how to work. If you hope to succeed in life on your
    own, you're going to have to know how to get a job
    done right. This will be the best boss you'll ever have!

2. Your help around the house is a small return on a
    huge investment these people have made in your
    life: childbirth, diaper changing, late night bottle
    feedings, trips to the zoo, vacations, free food,

clothes, entertainment, and schooling (they pay taxes for that). I could go on, but you get it!

3. Because Jesus told us to. In Matthew 5:41, He said that if someone asks you to go one mile for them, offer to go two. Our willingness to help others in a practical way is a testimony of God's goodness in our lives towards them.

3 WAYS HELPING YOUR PARENTS HELPS YOU

"What do I get out of this?" I'm glad you asked. Perhaps you get an allowance that you can point to as some form of payment for your help with the family chores. But maybe not. We've never had a regular allowance with any of our teenagers, but they've always worked very willingly because they care about our family and understand that rewards will come. So here are 3 ways helping out Mom and Dad will help you even more.

1. **Welcome to training camp for life's big leagues.** I'm so glad now that my parents instilled great work habits in me when I was a teenager. They gave me all that I would need to make my bosses happy and get me many raises along the way.

2. **You are sowing seed that will harvest in your own home one day.** I believe one of the reasons my 3 boys have always been good workers in our home, is that I was a good worker in my house. The Bible says in Galatians that God is never mocked and that *anytime* a seed of any kind is sown, you will reap in due season.

3. **Helping Mom and Dad gives you favor with them.** It won't be long until you really need something from your parents. Every willing, well-done work puts another good deposit in your favor account with them. Withdrawals are easier when you've put something in the bank.

7 REWARDS OF A DILIGENT WORKER

Many people seek to do the least they possibly have to at a job. What they fail to understand is that they are blocking the blessings of God from coming their way. Proverbs 21:5 assures us that the plans of the diligent will lead to plenty, while those who are hasty in their work will find poverty. Here are 7 rewards of the diligent worker.

1. **Promotion.** Hard work will be rewarded with higher positions of responsibility.

2. **Recognition.** A diligent person will stand out from the crowd, acknowledged by many.

3. **Wealth.** Companies and organizations will pay good money to those who do their job well.

4. **Respect.** You will gain esteem from your friends, your family, your peers, and your community.

5. **Opportunity.** You will find yourself becoming very valuable to others who will open new doors for you to walk through.

6. **Influence.** You will earn the privilege of teaching, training, and mentoring those who will want to learn from your success.

7. **Fullfillment.** You'll never have to live with regrets, wondering what you could have accomplished if you had only given your best.

4 SECRETS TO MAKE WORK GO FAST

Isn't that the hard thing about a job, that it seems to take forever? How come when you do something you enjoy, like sports, shopping, or hanging with friends, time just flies, and when you have to work in the yard for 2 hours, time almost goes backwards! Help is on the way. Check out these secrets to move that second hand around like a sprinter.

1. **Great mental preparation.** Don't approach work with visions of how long and bad it's going to be. "I'm going to get this job done and have a good time doing it!" This is the kind of mentality that will speed every-thing up.

2. **Slice your work up into smaller parts.** Don't sit there thinking about everything at once. Concentrate on cutting the front yard grass first. Now let's attack the

back yard. Okay, now I can get the weed eater out. One part at a time and you won't feel overwhelmed.

3. **Create personal competitions.** Try to figure out an easier or better way to get a job done. How can you do it faster without sacrificing quality? When you create challenges for yourself, you tend to forget about the time.

4. **Quit looking at your watch every 22 seconds!**

5 QUALITIES OF A JOB WELL DONE

It's not enough just to do a job. It's important that you do it well. In the work world, when you don't do a job well, you get to do it again, which takes even longer. Or you get fired. This, by the way, is not good. So you might as well figure out how to do work that makes people happy.

1. **Do all you do with joy.** Be happy, or at least force a smile on your face and fake it!

2. **Start strong.** Get started on time, and do the hardest stuff first while you have an abundance of energy.

3. **On each part of the job, ask yourself, "Is this the best I can do, or am I trying to get by with as little as possible?"** You know what the answer should be.

4. **Always look to add a little extra.** It may take 5 or 10 extra minutes, but do more than you were asked to do. "Oh yeah, Mom, I took out the trash too," are beautiful words to hear.

5. **Finish what you start.** Do a thorough check. Is everything done? Did I put my tools away? A job well done is a job that is complete.

[STRATEGIES]

3 MARKS OF PROUD PARENTS

I don't know that I've ever met a teenager who didn't want their parents to be proud of them. There's no one who knows you better than your mom and dad. If you can make them proud of your character and accomplishments, well done! Here are 3 goals to aspire to as a son or daughter.

1. **They look forward to taking you out in public.**
    It may be a restaurant, an event, or something else, but proud parents look for opportunities to spend extra time with you and show the world what a great kid they have.

2. **You become the topic of every conversation**
    (not because of trouble you've gotten into). Proud parents can't wait to brag on you to their friends and

neighbors. They've had a part in seeing you grow up and are thrilled to see you succeed.

3. **They want to help you fulfill your dreams.**
   When you've worked hard to please Mom and Dad, their natural desire will be to do anything in their ability to assist you in reaching your goals in life.

5 SCRIPTURES TO PRAY OVER YOUR FAMILY

Your family may be entirely Christians, or perhaps you have some who have yet to make Jesus Christ Lord of their lives. Either way, there are several Scriptures that pertain to family that you can begin praying in faith over each one. Here are five Scriptures.

1. "And you, fathers, do not provoke your children to wrath, but bring them up in the training and admonition of the Lord" (Eph. 6:4). Pray for your mom and dad to have patience in teaching and correcting you in righteousness.

2. "That the God of our Lord Jesus Christ, the Father of glory, may give to you the spirit of wisdom and revelation in the knowledge of Him" (Eph. 1:17). Pray that

your family members will have God's wisdom and understanding in all their decisions.

3. "And if it seems evil to you to serve the Lord, choose for yourselves this day whom you will serve, whether the gods which your fathers served that were on the other side of the River, or the gods of the Amorites, in whose land you dwell. But as for me and my house, we will serve the Lord" (Josh. 24:15). Pray and confess boldly that every person in your household is going to serve the Lord.

4. "So they said, 'Believe on the Lord Jesus Christ, and you will be saved, you and your household'" (Acts 16:31). Pray and believe God for the salvation of each member of your family.

5. "The righteous man walks in his integrity; his children are blessed after him" (Prov. 20:7). Pray for your parents to walk in truth and integrity, and for the blessing of God to be upon your entire family.

5 HABITS OF HAPPY TEENAGERS

God wants you to be happy and enjoy life. That doesn't mean you will never experience trials or tough times. Here are 5 habits you can develop as a young person that will cause you to keep your joy through even the darkest hours.

1. **Regularly reading and meditating (thinking and pondering) on God's Word.** (Ps. 119:105.) This will energize your joy!

2. **Steadily communing with God.** "Communion" comes from the word "communicate." That's it! Talk to God, praise Him, and give Him your requests and cares.

3. **Vision thinking.** Find out what God has gifted you in. Take time to seek Him for your career and ambitions. Take one step at a time as you grow to get there.

4. **Singing a good song aloud!** God made us to sing. Not all of us sound that good, but it doesn't matter. Find songs and worship music that inspire you for good, and sing! (Ps. 95:1.)

5. **Attending church weekly.** Stay connected to good friends, strong mentors, and caring pastors who will help you stay on track.

3 WAYS TO DEAL WITH TOUGH PARENTS

Parents aren't perfect. I know this because I am one. I've made mistakes in raising my kids, and I am the first to admit it to them when I've missed the mark. Even so, there are some parents who are really tough to deal with and are perhaps too hard on their kids. Here are some ways to handle parents who may be extremely difficult to get along with.

1. **Practice a soft answer.** The Bible says that a soft answer turns away wrath and anger. (Prov. 15:1.) Learn to hold your tongue and your temper, even when a parent does not. Do your best to set an example of patience and gentleness.

2. **Communicate well.** Be sure that you never leave a parent in the dark about what you're doing, where you're going, or when you're planning to do something.

Practice the "no surprise" rule. And learn to ask, rather than tell or demand. Give them the satisfaction of granting you permission, even on things you may take for granted.

3. **Don't become a victim of physical abuse.** If you have a parent who has become violent, constantly hitting you or beating you up physically, please let someone know who can help you. (I'm not talking about getting spankings while growing up.) Get help from a family member you trust or perhaps a church pastor or school counselor.

4 WAYS TO TELL PARENTS "THANK YOU"

I believe one of the greatest character traits that you can develop in your life is appreciation and gratefulness towards others. It's important that you find practical ways to show gratitude to someone who has been a blessing to you. Nothing warms my heart more as a father than when one of my boys takes the time to tell Cathy and me thanks for something we've done for them. Here are some ways you can say thanks.

1. **A card.** Take the time to write out your feelings towards your parents, accounting for the specific things they've done that you are grateful for.

2. **A gift.** It doesn't have to be expensive. Maybe it's a gift certificate to their favorite restaurant or store. A small sacrifice of finances on your part communicates a big message to Mom and Dad.

3. **Unexpected work.** Do something around the house you weren't asked to do: the trash, the dishes, the yard—whatever. Tell them you just wanted to find a way to say thanks.

4. **Go ahead and tell them.** Say it out loud and say it whenever they've done something good for you. A good meal. Permission to use the car. A night at the movies. Tell them thanks!

PRAYER OF SALVATION

God loves you—no matter who you are, no matter what your past. God loves you so much that He gave His one and only begotten Son for you. The Bible tells us that "…whoever believes in him shall not perish but have eternal life" (John 3:16 NIV). Jesus laid down His life and rose again so that we could spend eternity with Him in heaven and experience His absolute best on earth. If you would like to receive Jesus into your life, say the following prayer out loud and mean it from your heart.

Heavenly Father, I come to You admitting that I am a sinner. Right now, I choose to turn away from sin, and I ask You to cleanse me of all unrighteousness. I believe that Your Son, Jesus, died on the cross to take away my sins. I also believe that He rose again from the dead so that I might be forgiven of my sins and made righteous through faith in Him. I call upon the name of Jesus Christ to be the Savior and Lord of my life. Jesus, I choose to follow You and ask that You fill me with the power of the Holy Spirit. I declare that right now I am a child of God. I am free from sin and full of the righteousness of God. I am saved in Jesus' name. Amen.

If you prayed this prayer to receive Jesus Christ as your Savior for the first time, please contact us on the Web at **www.harrisonhouse.com** to receive a free book.

Or you may write to us at:

Harrison House

P.O. Box 35035

Tulsa, Oklahoma 74153

MEET BLAINE BARTEL

Blaine Bartel is one of America's premiere leadership specialists. Blaine served as Oneighty®'s Youth Pastor for 7 years, helping it become America's largest local church youth ministry, reaching more than 2,500 students each week. He is now the National Director of Oneighty® and Associate Pastor of 12,000-member Church On The Move in Tulsa, Oklahoma. Blaine has served under his Pastor and mentor, Willie George, for more than 20 years. God has uniquely gifted him to teach local church staff and workers to thrive while faithfully serving the vision of their leader. Known for his creativity and respected for his achievement, Blaine uses the *Thrive* audio resource to equip thousands of church and youth leaders each month with principles, ideas, and strategies that work.

Past: Came to Christ at age 16 on the heels of the Jesus movement. While in pursuit of a professional freestyle skiing career, answered God's call to reach young people. Developed and hosted groundbreaking television series, *Fire by Nite*. Planted and pastored a growing church in Colorado Springs.

Passion: Summed up in three simple words, "Serving America's Future." Blaine's life quest is "to relevantly introduce the person of Jesus Christ to each new generation of young people, leaving footprints for future leaders to follow."

Personal: Still madly in love with his wife and partner of 22 years, Cathy. Raising 3 boys who love God: Jeremy—19, Dillon—17, Brock—15. Avid hockey player and fan, with a rather impressive Gretzky memorabilia collection.

To contact Blaine Bartel,

write:

bb blaine bartel
serving america's future

Blaine Bartel

Serving America's Future

P.O. Box 691923

Tulsa, OK 74169

E-mail: bbartel@churchonthemove.com

Or visit him on his Web site at:

www.blainebartel.com

To contact Oneighty®, write:

Oneighty®

P.O. Box 770

Tulsa, OK 74101

www.Oneighty.com

OTHER BOOKS BY BLAINE BARTEL

Ten Rules to Youth Ministry and Why Oneighty®
Breaks Them All

Oneighty® Devotional

every teenager's
little black book
on reaching your dreams

every teenager's
little black book
for athletes

every teenager's
little black book
of God's guarantees

every teenager's
little black book
on how to win a friend to christ

every teenager's
little black book
on sex and dating

every teenager's
little black book
on cash

every teenager's
little black book
on cool

every teenager's
little black book
of hard to find information

little black book
for graduates

Additional copies of this book

are available from your local bookstore.

Harrison House

Tulsa, Oklahoma

www.harrisonhouse.com

Fast. Easy. Convenient!

- ◆ New Book Information
- ◆ Look Inside the Book
- ◆ Press Releases
- ◆ Bestsellers

- ◆ Free E-News
- ◆ Author Biographies
- ◆ Upcoming Books
- ◆ Share Your Testimony

For the latest in book news and author information, please visit us on the Web at www.harrisonhouse.com. Get up-to-date pictures and details on all our powerful and life-changing products. Sign up for our e-mail newsletter, *Friends of the House,* and receive free monthly information on our authors and products including testimonials, author announcements, and more!

Harrison House—
Books That Bring Hope, Books That Bring Change

THE HARRISON HOUSE VISION

Proclaiming the truth and the power

Of the Gospel of Jesus Christ

With excellence;

Challenging Christians to

Live victoriously,

Grow spiritually,

Know God intimately.